Terence Donovan

image maker and innovator

Terence Donovan

image maker and innovator

CHRIS BEETLES GALLERY

8 & 10 Ryder Street St James's London SW1Y 6QB
Telephone 020 7839 7551 Facsimile 020 7839 1603
gallery@chrisbeetles.com www.chrisbeetles.com

© Chris Beetles Ltd 2007
8 & 10 Ryder Street
St James's
London
SW1Y 6QB

020 7839 7551
gallery@chrisbeetles.com
www.chrisbeetles.com

ISBN 978-1-905738-04-5

Compiled and edited by Giles Huxley-Parlour
Design by Jeremy Brook at Graphic Ideas
Colour separation and printing by BAS Printers

Contents

All prints are from the Estate of Terence Donovan

Introduction

Terence Donovan (1936-1996) came to prominence in London in the 1960s as part of a post-war renaissance in art, fashion, graphic design and photography. The energy of his fashion photographs and portraits, and the force of his personality, have assumed in the intervening years an almost folkloric significance. With David Bailey and Brian Duffy, photographers of a similar background and outlook, Donovan was perceived as a new force in British fashion photography. The three comprised a 'Black Trinity', according to Norman Parkinson, who found their methodology crude and their pictures at best 'unpolished'. Donovan was 23 when he opened his studio, Bailey the same age when his first substantial commission came from *Vogue*. Their early success heralded the era of the 'specialised hero', which *Vogue* and *Queen* magazines would reinforce – and mythologize – in print. Donovan's accredited appearance in a star-studded Bailey fashion shoot, for *Vogue* in 1961, was an early signifier that photographers were now the equal to television stars, comedians and theatre actors. Later, on screen, Michelangelo Antonioni's *Blow up* (1966) would strengthen the notion of photographer-as-cultural-icon.

Though they approached photography in distinct ways, the three – and others such as John Cowan – remain emblems for a decade of ambition, energy and opportunism. Cecil Beaton (like Parkinson, of the generation the three would eclipse) spoke, not entirely with approbation, of Donovan 'creating such a stir!' With hindsight, he went further: 'Donovan's young girls had no innocence and he somehow contrived to make them look as if they were wearing soiled underwear...' The new democratic nature of photography and its discomforting effect, was boosted by Duffy's triumphant assertion that 'before us, fashion photographers were tall, thin and camp. We're different. We're short, fat and heterosexual'.

As early as 1962, Donovan and Bailey were hailed as 'masters of the quick and vivid image' but, to many observers and collectors, it has become clear with the passage of time that Donovan's inventiveness continued into the following decades. He consolidated his success as a magazine photographer with a parallel career as a documentary filmmaker and with a body of self-motivated projects, such as idiosyncratic nude work and portraiture, landscape photography and, unexpectedly, the documentation of Judo. At the time, little of this reached a wide audience. However, he established himself as a maker of television commercials and pop videos, including that for *Addicted to Love* (1985) by Robert Palmer, considered to be one of the most influential and memorable videos ever made. In his later years, he developed a love of painting and exhibited vast abstract canvases inspired by Japanese calligraphy.

Donovan was born in East London on 14 September 1936, the son of Daniel Donovan, a lorry driver, and his wife Constance. His education was often disrupted. 'I spent most of the war', he once said, 'in the cab of a large lorry travelling round England.' However, he developed an interest in photography, which chimed with a golden age for black and white periodicals, notably *Picture Post* and *Lilliput*. Influenced by the documentary work of Bill Brandt, whose stark black and white photo-essays appeared in both magazines, Donovan brought urban realism to his early magazine and advertising work. His backdrop was the blitzed and cratered landscape of his East End youth, observing that here was 'a tough emptiness, a grittiness heightened by occasional pieces of rubbish rustling around in the wind.' While his contemporaries Don McCullin and Roger Mayne found this urban landscape conducive to pure reportorial photography, Donovan brought this grittiness to the depiction of clothes.

This reached an early apogee in a series of men's fashion pictures taken on the streets of London for *Man About Town*, published in 1961 and, for the same magazine a year later, a series of portraits *en deshabille* of the young actress Julie Christie in her London flat. The degree of informality brought to both was untypical of the time (and prompted Beaton's disapproval). The sense of unobserved scrutiny in the Christie portfolio – the actress' gaze rarely addressed the camera – appeared voyeuristic (a situation replicated later with the actress Sarah Miles). This approach was explored regularly in his magazine work and up until the 1990s remained a constant for magazines that sought a Donovan *imprimatur*.

Commercial exigencies as well as expediency for the photographer ensured that studio work was not neglected. As Donovan's reputation grew, and the financial rewards for commercial work increased, his milieu became more sophisticated and efficient. His studio was able to entertain three, occasionally four, sittings a day. By the 1980s it ran like clockwork, which occasionally gave his work a formulaic feel. However, the best examples repeated a *mise-en-scène* first formulated in the sixties. He had always avoided the vocabulary of exaggerated 'high fashion' postures in favour of a visual language taken from the streets and from the girls of his East End youth. This scrutiny of gesture and stance was, in his own words, a 'sort of working-class chic' and it stayed as part of his own vocabulary for almost his entire career.

In 1960 and 1961, again for *Man About Town*, he contributed two uncharacteristic though influential photo-essays that went on to inform his fashion work. For the first, 'The Lay About Life', he documented in grimy detail an artists' collective in Holland Park; for the second, he trailed a West End stripper for a day, from early morning until late at night. Both were downbeat, the latter conveying the pathos and loneliness of a nascent 'sex industry' and the former an almost forensic study of British domestic life lived on the margin. Both were a counterpoint in photographic stills to the prevailing cinematic wave of British 'Kitchen Sink' realism: Karel Reisz's *Saturday Night and Sunday Morning* was released a month before Donovan's

Holland Park photographs were published; Tony Richardson's *A Taste of Honey* two months after the 'Stripper' series. In spirit they appear closer to the domestic interiors and the windblown urban landscapes of 'new realist' painters such as John Bratby and Derrick Greaves.

These sets of pictures were enlightening and anomalous, for Donovan chose not to pursue 'straight' documentary work thereafter but concentrated even more firmly on fashion photography: 'I tend to reduce my reportage to graphics,' he explained later, 'I don't really want to report on life...I'm quite happy to see a girl scratching her nose in a coffee bar and translate that via a model.' This translation successfully found its way to the pages of less experimental magazines than *Man about Town*, chiefly *Vogue* and subsequently graphically powerful ones such as *Nova* and *The Sunday Times Colour Section*. The latter was almost an in-house magazine for a generation of British fashion and reportage photographers. It first appeared in February 1962 with a composite cover – by Bailey – very much in the spirit of Donovan's cinema *verité style*. Donovan himself was a contributor to the second issue.

Except for *Elle*, art directed by Peter Knapp, foreign magazines received Donovan's informal approach with coolness, and, as he very much depended upon them for a steady stream of assignments, this had to change. Thus, for French and Italian *Harper's Bazaar* particularly, Donovan chose a different tactic. He exaggerated – almost to the point of parody – the *hauteur* of the high-end glossy magazine. This instinct for the highly colourful, for an 'overdone glamour', existed concomitantly with an economy of style, and both kept him in demand from the 1970s to the mid-1990s. Sensing perhaps the inconsistencies in his approach to magazine work, that it was not 'pure', he exculpated himself by maintaining a distance from the fashion world: 'Fashion photography is an act of theatre, and I suppose you really have to love it...' But his ambivalent, sometimes querulous, attitude to fashion was pursued in two television documentaries on the twice-yearly Paris Collections.

Inevitably, Donovan brought these two distinct approaches to magazine portraiture too. His first photograph for *Vogue*, for example, a portrait of the conductor George Solti walking the streets of Covent Garden, is a skilful long-lens observation shot, but throughout the 1970s and 1980s and frequently for *Vogue*, he concentrated on the studio portrait, wherein any element of chance was, for the most part, removed. The results – most particularly a series of headshots of the comedians Max Wall, Norman Wisdom and the writer and wit Osbert Lancaster – are determinedly unflattering with no indulgence to the sitter's vanity or the 'look' of the magazine. From 1970, while continuing to shoot fashion for a variety of magazines, he explored in earnest the more lucrative field of advertising photography, also turning his hand to the moving image.

Donovan was at work until he died in November 1996. He had started preparatory work on the construction of a large studio in West London, while a series of portraits of contemporary musicians for *GQ* had renewed interest in his editorial work. His last *Vogue* commission was a portrait of the fashion designers Suzanne Clements and Inacio Ribeiro ('Clements Ribeiro') made just two weeks before he died and published posthumously.

Vintage prints of Donovan's fashion and portrait work, particularly those from the 1960s and 1970s, are rare. Even more so are 'signed' works. He belonged to the generation that never considered that there could ever be a market for what was essentially commercial photography, no matter how accomplished. Donovan's diffidence went further. As a working photographer he spurned compilations of his work or exhibitions of past highpoints, because, presumably, he felt the best was still to come. In his lifetime, he published only three books of his photographs. None was particularly historical nor any an anthology of his greatest moments and all were idiosyncratic. The first in 1964 *Women Throoo The Eyes Of Smudger Terence Donovan*, was a slim booklet of women he had recently photographed (including several pictures of Julie Christie and Sarah Miles, and out-takes from the 'Stripper' series). *Glances*, the second, coming nearly twenty years later in 1983, was a book of nudes and the third and last, *Fighting Judo* from 1985, the most unexpected: a 'blow-by-blow' manual of judo moves. (Donovan was a black belt 1st dan.)

Unsurprisingly, there are few signed prints in the Donovan archive. However, what has surfaced is a cache of contact photographs, curiously authenticated. For the decade 1959 to the end of the 1960s, Donovan separated from his contact sheets, and invariably printed up to the standard of a finished print, those images he favoured for publication – promptly stabbing them clean through with the point of a pencil. This is surely a forceful stamp of authorship and authority from one of British photography's foremost identities. And one whom, it must be said, made strenuous efforts to avoid a conventional photographic legacy.

Robin Muir
2007

Modern Prints

These prints are from a limited
edition of 50, strictly controlled by
Chris Beetles Ltd and The Terence
Donovan Estate.

1. Advertising shoot for Hoovermatic, London, 1961

Photographer's estate stamp on reverse
Silver gelatin print
14 x 20 inches
From a limited edition of 50

London, 1 November 1961
Models: Sheila Macklin and Tim Davis
Agency: Erwin Wasey
Client: Hoovermatic

2. Miss Allen and Children, 1959
Advertising shoot for George
Newnes

Photographer's estate stamp on reverse
Silver gelatin print, 18 x 18 inches
From a limited edition of 50
Literature: Diana Donovan and David
Hillman (editors), *Terence Donovan: The
Photographs*, London: Little Brown &
Co, 2000 (unpaginated).
Another print of this image was
exhibited at *The Eye That Never Sleeps –
Terence Donovan – London Photographs*,
Museum of London, 17 March –
1 August 1999

London, 3 April 1959
Client: George Newnes
Model: Miss Allen and Children

**3. Kitchen, Notting Hill Gate, 1959
'The Lay About Life' photo essay**

Photographer's estate stamp on reverse
Silver gelatin print, 8½ x 20 inches
From a limited edition of 50
Illustrated: *Man About Town*, December
1960, 'The Lay About Life'
Literature: Diana Donovan and David

Hillman (editors), *Terence Donovan: The
Photographs*, London: Little Brown & Co, 2000
(unpaginated)

Another print of this image was exhibited at
*The Eye That Never Sleeps – Terence Donovan –
London Photographs*, Museum of London,
17 March – 1 August 1999

Notting Hill Gate, London, 3 April 1959

4. Graffiti, Notting Hill Gate, 1960
'The Lay About Life' photo essay

Photographer's estate stamp on reverse
Silver gelatin print, 18 x 18 inches
From a limited edition of 50
Illustrated: *Man About Town*, December
1960, 'The Lay About Life'
Literature: Diana Donovan and David
Hillman (editors), *Terence Donovan: The*
Photographs, London: Little Brown & Co,
2000 (unpaginated)

Another print of this image was exhibited at
The Eye That Never Sleeps – Terence Donovan
– London Photographs, Museum of London,

17 March–1 August 1999
Notting Hill Gate, London, 10 October 1960
Client: *Man About Town*

5. Payphone, Notting Hill Gate, 1960
'The Lay About Life' photo essay

Photographer's estate stamp on reverse
Silver gelatin print, 18 x 18 inches
From a limited edition of 50
Illustrated: *Man About Town*, December
1960, 'The Lay About Life'
Literature: Diana Donovan and David
Hillman (editors), *Terence Donovan: The*
Photographs, London: Little Brown & Co,
2000 (unpaginated).

Another print of this image was exhibited at
The Eye That Never Sleeps – Terence Donovan
– London Photographs, Museum of London,

17 March – 1 August 1999
Notting Hill Gate, London, 10 October 1960
Client: *Man About Town*

6. 'The Secrets of an Agent' I, 1961
Men's fashion for *Man About Town*

Photographer's estate stamp on reverse
Silver gelatin print, 18 x 18 Inches
From a limited edition of 50
Illustrated: *Man About Town*, May 1961,
'The Secrets of an Agent'
Another print of this image was
exhibited at *The Eye That Never Sleeps* –

Terence Donovan – London Photographs,
Museum of London, 17 March –
1 August 1999

London, 6 March 1961
Model: Peter Begarty
Client: *Man About Town*

7. 'The Secrets of an Agent' II, 1961
Men's fashion for *Man About Town*

Photographer's estate stamp on reverse
Silver gelatin print, 18 x 18 inches
From a limited edition of 50
Illustrated: *Man About Town*, May 1961,
'The Secrets of an Agent'
Literature: Martin Harrison,
Appearances: Fashion Photography Since
1945, London: Cape, 1991
Another print of this image was
exhibited at *The Eye That Never Sleeps –*
Terence Donovan – London Photographs,
Museum of London, 17 March –
1 August 1999

London, 6 March 1961
Model: Peter Begarty
Client: *Man About Town*

8. 'The Secrets of an Agent' III, 1961
Men's fashion for *Man About Town*

Photographer's estate stamp on reverse
Silver gelatin print, 18 x 18 inches
From a limited edition of 50
Illustrated: *Man About Town*, May 1961,
'The Secrets of an Agent'
Another print of this image was

exhibited at *The Eye That Never Sleeps –*
Terence Donovan – London Photographs,
Museum of London, 17 March –
1 August 1999

London, 6 March 1961
Model: Peter Begarty
Client: *Man About Town*

9. Advertising shoot for Terylene, 1960

Photographer's estate stamp on reverse
Digital bromide print, 18 x 18 inches
From a limited edition of 50
Literature: Diana Donovan and David
Hillman (editors), *Terence Donovan: The
Photographs*, London: Little Brown & Co,
2000 (unpaginated)

London, 10 March 1960
Model: Peter Anthony
Agency: Mather & Crowther
Client: Terylene

10. 'Thermodynamic', 1960
Fashion shoot for *Man About Town*

Photographer's estate stamp on reverse
Silver gelatin print, 18 x 18 inches
Illustrated: *Man About Town*, January
1961, 'Thermodynamic'
Literature: Martin Harrison,
*Appearances: Fashion Photography Since
1945*, London: Cape, 1991. Diana
Donovan and David Hillman (editors),
Terence Donovan: The Photographs,

London: Little Brown & Co, 2000
(unpaginated)
Another print of this image was
exhibited at *The Eye That Never Sleeps –
Terence Donovan – London Photographs*,
Museum of London, 17 March –
1 August 1999

Grove Road Power Station, London,
31 October 1960
Model: Tim Davies
Client: *Man About Town*

11. Norman Parkinson, 1960

Photographer's estate stamp on reverse
Silver gelatin print, 18 x 18 inches
From a limited edition of 50

London, 22 December 1960
Client: *The Sunday Times*

12. Sean Connery, 1962
Advertising shoot for Smirnoff Vodka

London, 1 January 1962
Agency: Mather & Crowther
Client: Smirnoff Vodka

Photographer's estate stamp on reverse
Silver gelatin print, 20 x 24 inches
From a limited edition of 50

13. Kingsley Amis, 1960

London, 18 August 1960
Client: *Man About Town*

Photographer's estate stamp on reverse
Silver gelatin print, 18 x 18 inches
From a limited edition of 50

14. Celia Hammond, 1961

Photographer's estate stamp on reverse
Silver gelatin print, 18 x 18 inches
From a limited edition of 50
Literature: Diana Donovan and David
Hillman (editors), *Terence Donovan: The
Photographs*, London: Little Brown &
Co, 2000 (unpaginated)

Another print of this image was
exhibited at *The Eye That Never Sleeps –
Terence Donovan – London Photographs*,
Museum of London, 17 March –
1 August 1999

London, 18 December 1961
Test Shots

15. Celia Hammond, 1962
Fashion shoot for *Queen*

Photographer's estate stamp on reverse
Silver gelatin print, 20 × 24 inches
From a limited edition of 50
Illustrated: *Queen*, 25 September 1963
Literature: Martin Harrison,
*Appearances: Fashion Photography Since
1945*, London: Cape, 1991
Diana Donovan and David Hillman

(editors), *Terence Donovan: The Photographs*,
London: Little Brown & Co, 2000
(unpaginated)

Another print of this image was exhibited at
*The Eye That Never Sleeps – Terence Donovan
– London Photographs*, Museum of London,
17 March – 1 August 1999

London, 28 August 1963
Model: Celia Hammond
Client: *Queen*

16. Julie Christie, 1962

Photographer's estate stamp on reverse
Silver gelatin print, 20 x 24 inches
From a limited edition of 50

London, 14 May 1962
Client: *Man About Town*

17. Julie Christie, 1962

Photographer's estate stamp on reverse
Silver gelatin print, 20 x 24 inches
From a limited edition of 50
Illustrated: *Terence Donovan, Women Throooo The Eyes Of Smudger*,
London: Kynoch Press, 1964
Literature: Diana Donovan and David Hillman (editors), *Terence Donovan: The Photographs*, London: Little Brown & Co, 2000 (unpaginated).
Another print of this image was exhibited at *The Eye That Never Sleeps – Terence Donovan – London Photographs*, Museum of London, 17 March – 1 August 1999

London, 14 May 1962
Client: *Man About Town*

18. Claudia Cardinale, 1962

Photographer's estate stamp on
reverse
Silver gelatin print, 20 x 14 inches
From a limited edition of 50
Illustrated: Terence Donovan,

*Women Throooo The Eyes Of
Smudger,* London: Kynoch Press,
1964

London, 26 February 1962
Client: *Man About Town*

19. Mary Quant, 1963

Photographer's estate stamp on reverse
Silver gelatin print, 24 x 14 inches
From a limited edition of 50
Literature: Diana Donovan and David Hillman (editors), *Terence Donovan: The Photographs*, London: Little Brown & Co, 2000 (unpaginated)

London, 18 July 1963
Client: Bazaar

20. Sophia Loren Smoking, 1963
Taken on the set of Anthony Mann's
The Fall Of The Roman Empire

Photographer's estate stamp on reverse
Silver gelatin print, 15 x 20 inches
From a limited edition of 50
Illustrated: Terence Donovan, *Women Throooo
The Eyes Of Smudger*, London: Kynoch Press,
1964

Literature: Diana Donovan & David
Hillman (editors), *Terence Donovan: The
Photographs*, London: Little Brown &
Co, 2000 (unpaginated)

Spain, 19 – 22 May 1963
Client: *Queen* (unpublished)

21. Sophia Loren, 1963
Taken on the set of Anthony Mann's
The Fall Of The Roman Empire

Photographer's estate stamp on reverse
Silver gelatin print, 14 x 20 inches
From a limited edition of 50

Spain, 19 – 22 May 1963
Client: *Queen* (unpublished)

22. Thirty-nine jazz musicians, 1962
From left to right. Top row: Bruce Turner, Tony Milliner, Al Fairweather, Johnny Burch, Don Rendell, Tony Archer, Tony Russell, Les Condon, Gus Galbraith. Second row: Sandy Brown, Dick Heckstall-Smith, Coleridge Goodge, Wally Fawkes, Wally Wright, Pete King. Third row: Brian Lemmon, Brian Prudence. Bottom row: Dave Davies, Laurie Morgan, Herman Wilson, George Melly, Chris Staunton, Buzz Green, Tony Kinsey, Peter McGurk, Dudley Moore, Michael Garrick, Morris Gaurensky, Vic Ash, Gordon Beck, Brian Dee, Graham Bond, Jimmy Deucher, Alan

Ganley, Tubby Hayes, Benny Green, Stan Robinson, Colin Perbrook, Bill Eyden.

Photographer's estate stamp on reverse
Digital LAMBDA print, 18 x 36 inches
From a limited edition of 50
Illustrated: *Queen*, 24 April 1962

Another print of this image was exhibited at *The Eye That Never Sleeps – Terence Donovan – London Photographs*, Museum of London, 17 March – 1 August 1999

London, 29 March 1962
Client: *Queen*

23. Advertising shoot for Black & White Whisky, 1964

Photographer's estate stamp on reverse
Silver gelatin print, 18 x 18 inches
From a limited edition of 50
Literature: Diana Donovan and David Hillman
(editors), *Terence Donovan: The Photographs*,
London: Little Brown & Co, 2000 (unpaginated)

Another print of this image was exhibited at
*The Eye That Never Sleeps – Terence Donovan –
London Photographs*, Museum of London
17 March – 1 August 1999

London, 23 April 1964
Agency: GSR
Client: Black & White Whisky

24. Tony Hancock, 1963
Advertising shoot for The British
Railways Board

Photographer's estate stamp on reverse
Digital bromide print, 18 x 18 inches
From a limited edition of 50
Literature: Diana Donovan and David Hillman

(editors), *Terence Donovan: The Photographs*,
London: Little Brown & Co, 2000 (unpaginated)

Waterloo Station, London, 11 September 1963
Agency: WSC
Client: The British Railways Board

25. Advertising shoot for Woollands I, 1965

Photographer's estate stamp on reverse
Silver gelatin print, 18 x 18 inches
From a limited edition of 50

26. Advertising shoot for Woollands II, 1965

Photographer's estate stamp on reverse
Silver gelatin print, 18 x 18 inches
From a limited edition of 50

Paris & London, July & 11 August 1965
Agency: S & W
Client: Woollands

27. Karen Jensen & Ahmed, 1965
Fashion shoot for *Queen*

Photographer's estate stamp on reverse
Silver gelatin print, 18 x 18 inches
From a limited edition of 50
Literature: Diana Donovan and David

Hillman (editors), *Terence Donovan: The Photographs*, London: Little Brown & Co, 2000 (unpaginated)

Models: Karen Jensen and Ahmed
Client: *Queen*

28. Karen Jensen, 1965
Fashion shoot for *Queen*

Model: Karen Jensen
Client: *Queen*

Photographer's estate stamp on reverse
Silver gelatin print, 18 x 18 inches
From a limited edition of 50

29. Twiggy, 1966

Photographer's estate stamp on reverse
Silver gelatin print, 18 x 18 inches
From a limited edition of 50
Illustrated: *Woman's Mirror*, 27 August 1966,
'Sundae Best'

30. Terence Stamp, 1966
On the set of John Schlesinger's *Far From*
The Madding Crowd

Photographer's estate stamp on reverse
Silver gelatin print, 18 x 18 inches
Illustrated: *Vogue*, July 1967, 'Madding Crowd
assembled'

Literature: Diana Donovan and David
Hillman (editors), *Terence Donovan: The
Photographs*, London: Little Brown & Co,
2000 (unpaginated)
Another print of this image was exhibited at
*The Eye That Never Sleeps – Terence Donovan
– London Photographs*, Museum of London,
17 March – 1 August 1999

31. Marianne Faithfull, 1966

Photographer's estate stamp on reverse
Silver gelatin print, 14 x 20 inches
From a limited edition of 50

London, 24 June 1966

32. Marianne Faithfull, 1966
Advertising shoot for Selfridges

Photographer's estate stamp on reverse
Silver gelatin print, 20 x 25 inches
From a limited edition of 50

London, 27 July 1966
Agency: CD
Client: Selfridges

33. Fashion shoot, 1966

Photographer's estate stamp on reverse
Silver gelatin print, 18 x 18 inches
From a limited edition of 50

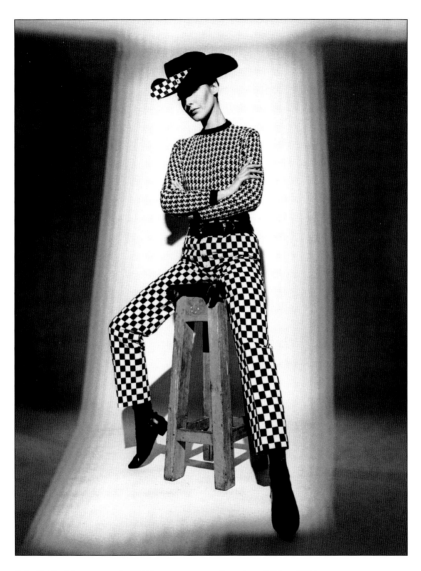

34. Celia Hammond, 1966
Fashion shoot for *Harper's Bazaar*

London, 5 May 1966
Client: *Harper's Bazaar*

Photographer's estate stamp on reverse
Silver gelatin print, 20 x 15 inches
From a limited edition of 50

35. Joanna Lumley, 1966
Fashion shoot for Selfridges

Stamped with photographer's estate stamp
on reverse
Silver gelatin print, 18 x 18 inches

London, 25 April 1966
Model: Joanna Lumley
Client: Selfridges

36. Josephine Florent, 1978

Photographer's estate stamp on reverse
Silver gelatin print, 20 x 24 inches
From a limited edition of 50
Illustrated: Terence Donovan, *Glances,*
London: Michael Joseph, 1983, plate 58
Literature: Diana Donovan and David
Hillman (editors), *Terence Donovan:
The Photographs,* London: Little
Brown & Co, 2000 (unpaginated)
Another print of this image was
exhibited at *The Eye That Never
Sleeps – Terence Donovan – London
Photographs,* Museum of London,
17 March – 1 August 1999

37. Nude, 1964

Photographer's estate stamp on
reverse
Silver gelatin print, 20 x 24 inches
From a limited edition of 50
Literature: Diana Donovan and

David Hillman (editors), *Terence
Donovan: The Photographs*,
London: Little Brown & Co, 2000
(unpaginated)

38. Nude, 1967

Photographer's estate stamp on reverse
Silver gelatin print, 20 x 24 inches
From a limited edition of 50
Literature: Diana Donovan and David Hillman (editors), *Terence Donovan: The Photographs*, London: Little Brown & Co, 2000 (unpaginated)

London, 26 October 1967

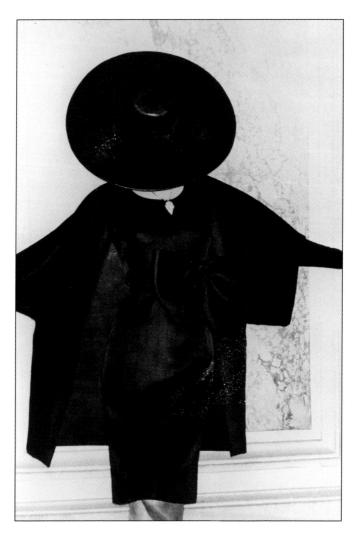

39. Danielle Noel, 1965
Fashion shoot for *Queen*

Photographer's estate stamp on reverse
Silver gelatin print, 20 x 24 inches
From a limited edition of 50
Literature: Diana Donovan and David Hillman (editors), *Terence Donovan: The Photographs*, London: Little Brown & Co, 2000 (unpaginated)

Paris, 12 March 1965
Model: Danielle Noel
Client: *Queen*

40. Celia Hammond, circa 1976

Photographer's estate stamp on reverse
Digital bromide print, 18 x 18 inches
From a limited edition of 50
Literature: Diana Donovan & David
Hillman (editors), *Terence Donovan: The
Photographs*, London: Little Brown & Co,
2000 (unpaginated)
Another print of this image was
exhibited at *The Eye That Never Sleeps –
Terence Donovan – London Photographs*,
Museum of London, 17 March –
1 August 1999

41. Margaret Morris, 1969

Photographer's estate stamp on reverse
Silver gelatin print, 18 x 18 inches
From a limited edition of 50
Illustrated: *Nova*, November 1969

Literature: Diana Donovan and David Hillman
(editors), *Terence Donovan: The Photographs*,
London: Little Brown & Co, 2000 (unpaginated)

42. Daisy Donovan, circa 1978

Photographer's estate stamp on reverse
Silver gelatin print, 20 x 15 inches
From a limited edition of 50
Literature: Diana Donovan and David
Hillman (editors), *Terence Donovan: The Photographs*, London: Little Brown & Co, 2000 (unpaginated)

London, circa 1978

43. Girl on a bed, 1982

Photographer's estate stamp on reverse
Silver gelatin print, 18 x 18 inches
Illustrated: Terence Donovan, *Glances*,
London: Michael Joseph, 1983, Plate 4

Another print of this image was
exhibited at *The Eye That Never Sleeps –
Terence Donovan – London Photographs*,
Museum of London, 17 March –
1 August 1999

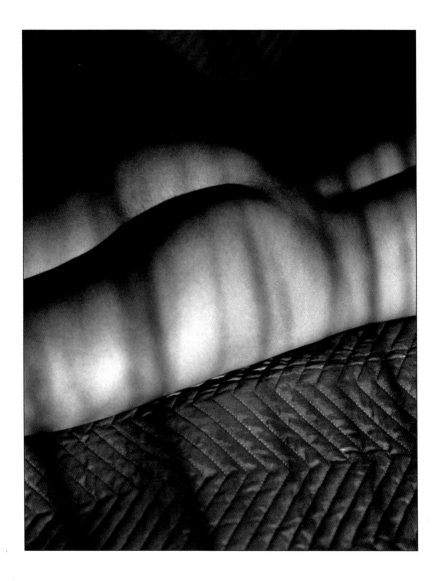

44. Nude study, cropped, circa 1983

Photographer's estate stamp on reverse
Silver gelatin print, 20 x 25 inches
Illustrated: Terence Donovan, *Glances*,
London: Michael Joseph, 1983, plate 23

45. Policewoman, 1983

Photographer's estate stamp on reverse
Silver gelatin print, 18 x 18 inches
Illustrated: Terence Donovan, *Glances*,
London: Michael Joseph, 1983, Plate 17

Literature: Diana Donovan & David
Hillman (Editors), *Terence Donovan: The
Photographs*, London: Little Brown & Co,
2000 (unpaginated)

46. Soldier, 1983

Photographer's estate stamp on reverse
Silver gelatin print, 20 × 16 inches
Illustrated: Terence Donovan, *Glances*,
London: Michael Joseph, 1983, Plate 45

47. Fashion shoot for *Vogue*, 1983

Photographer's estate stamp on reverse
Silver gelatin print, 18 x 18 inches
Illustrated: *Vogue*, December 1983, 'High Society'
Literature: Diana Donovan and David Hillman
(editors), *Terence Donovan: The Photographs*,
London: Little Brown & Co, 2000 (unpaginated)

London, 9 September 1983

48. Room 251, Park Lane Hotel, London, 1988

Photographer's estate stamp on reverse
Silver gelatin print, 20 x 13 inches

Room 251, Park Lane Hotel
London, 6 June 1988

Camera: Fujica 6 x 8
Film: PX 120
Aperture: F 5.63
Speed: 1/4 Second
Model: Michelle Geddes
Make up: Martin Pretorious
Client: Italian *Harper's Bazaar*

49. Francis Bacon, 1990

Photographer's estate stamp on reverse
Silver gelatin print, 13 x 20 inches
Literature: Diana Donovan and David Hillman
(editors), *Terence Donovan: The Photographs*,
London: Little Brown & Co, 2000 (unpaginated)

Chelsea, London, 1 September 1990

50. Nude, 1990

Photographer's estate stamp on reverse
Silver gelatin print, 13 x 20 inches
Literature: Diana Donovan and David Hillman
(editors), *Terence Donovan: The Photographs*,
London: Little Brown & Co, 2000 (unpaginated)

51. Cindy Crawford, 1988

Photographer's estate stamp on reverse
Silver gelatin print, 20 x 15 inches
Illustrated: *Vogue*, August 1988, 'Cut to
the Night'
Literature: Diana Donovan and David
Hillman (editors), *Terence Donovan: The
Photographs*, London: Little Brown & Co,
2000 (unpaginated)

Bourdon St, London, 26 April 1988
Hair: Nicky Clarke
Client: *Vogue*

52. Bryan Ferry, 1996

Photographer's estate stamp on reverse
Silver gelatin print, 20 x 14 inches
Literature: Diana Donovan and David Hillman (Editors), *Terence Donovan: The Photographs*, London: Little Brown & Co, 2000 (unpaginated)
A variant of this image was featured in *GQ* magazine, July 1996, in an article entitled 'National Anthems'

Bourdon St, London, 21 June 1996
Camera: Fuji 6 x 8
Client: *GQ*

53 Sir Ralph Richardson, Lord Olivier & Alec Guinness, 1980

Photographer's estate stamp on reverse
Silver gelatin print, 20 x 15 inches
Literature: Diana Donovan and David Hillman (editors), *Terence*

Donovan: The Photographs, London: Little Brown & Co, 2000 (unpaginated)
Another print of this image was exhibited at *The Eye That Never Sleeps – Terence Donovan – London Photographs*, Museum of London, 17 March – 1 August 1999

Client: British *Vogue* (unpublished)

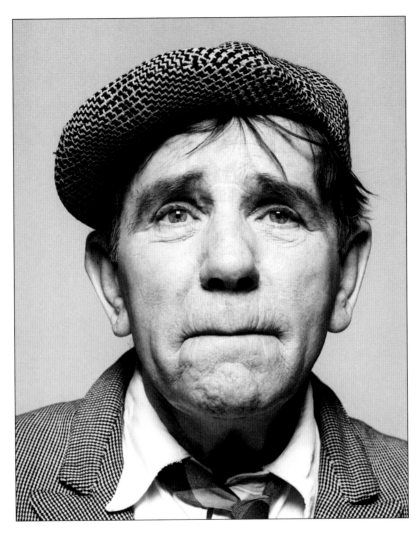

**54. Norman Wisdom, 1988
Advertising shoot for British
Telecom**

Photographer's estate stamp on reverse
Silver gelatin print, 20 x 16 inches
Literature: Diana Donovan and David
Hillman (Editors), *Terence Donovan: The*

Photographs, London: Little Brown &
Co, 2000 (unpaginated)

Bourdon St, London, 5 October 1988
Agency: J Walter Thompson
Client: British Telecom

55. Soccer players, circa 1980

Photographer's estate stamp on reverse
Digital bromide print, 13 x 20 inches
Literature: Diana Donovan and David Hillman
(editors), *Terence Donovan: The Photographs*,
London: Little Brown & Co, 2000 (unpaginated)

56. Eastbourne, 1996

Photographer's estate stamp on reverse
Digital bromide print, 13 x 20 inches
Literature: Diana Donovan and David Hillman
(editors), *Terence Donovan: The Photographs*,
London: Little Brown & Co, 2000 (unpaginated)

Contact Prints

Contact prints are created in the darkroom by laying strips of negatives flat on photographic paper, then exposing them to light in a normal enlarger. This process results in positives from which photographers can more easily choose the best images from a shoot.

Donovan indicated his preferred images by stabbing them with a pencil, after which they were separated and stored for future reference. These unique examples were found in the archive and date from the days immediately following each of these classic assignments.

57. Advertising shoot for Lurex, 1959   London, 18 August 1959
Model: Helen Bunney

Inscribed '150' on reverse
Unique silver gelatin contact print
2½ x 2½ inches

58. Fashion shoot for *Harper's Bazaar*, 1964

London, 1 April 1964
Client: *Harper's Bazaar*

Inscribed '1401/2' on reverse
Unique silver gelatin contact print
2½ x 2½ inches

59. Advertising shoot for Lactron, 1959

Inscribed '107' on reverse
Unique silver gelatin contact print
2½ x 2¼ inches

London, 18 August 1959
Model: Margaret Lorraine
Agency: Gee Advertising
Client: Lactron Brochure

60. Advertising shoot for Hoovermatic, 1961

Inscribed 'NB Keep as much light & detail in trouser fabric as possible'
Inscribed '875-102' on reverse
Unique silver gelatin contact print
2¼ x 2¼ inches

London, 29 December 1961
Models: Sheila Macklin &
Celia Hammond
Agency: Erwin Wasey
Client: Hoovermatic

61. Rose leaves with black spot, 1963

Inscribed '1197/1' on reverse
Unique silver gelatin contact print
5 x 4 inches

London, 14 May 1963
Agency: Y & R
Client: De La Rue

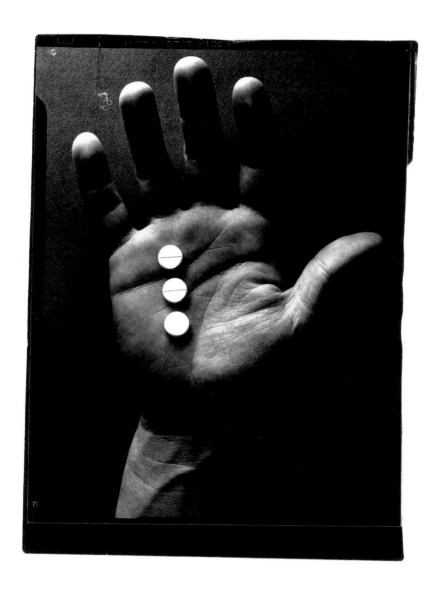

62. Advertising shoot for Roche, 1965

Inscribed '1714/3' on reverse
Unique silver gelatin contact print
5½ x 4 inches

London, 3 December 1965
Model: Tim Davis
Client: Roche

63. Jill Kennington, 1963
Advertising shoot for Tricel

Inscribed '1155-14' on reverse
Unique silver gelatin contact print
2½ x 2½ inches

London, 25 & 26 February 1963
Model: Jill Kennington
Agency: GSR
Client: Tricel

64. Shoe Study, 1962

Inscribed '1115-4' on reverse
Unique silver gelatin contact print
2½ x 2¼ inches

65. Fashion shoot for *Man About Town*, 1960

London, 30 August 1960
Client: *Man About Town*

Inscribed '461' on reverse
Unique silver gelatin contact print
2¼ x 2¼ inches

66. Celia Hammond, 1963
Advertising shoot for Bourneville

Inscribed 'Neg to Anglia T.V. 2.8.67'
and '1231/101' on reverse
Unique silver gelatin contact print
2½ x 2½ inches

London, 16 July 1963
Model: Celia Hammond
Agency: LPE
Client: Bourneville

67, 68. Celia Hammond, 1963
Fashion shoot for *Harper's Bazaar*

Two unique silver gelatin contact prints
One inscribed '1111-32' on reverse and
the other inscribed '1111-30' on reverse
Each 2½ x 2½ inches

London, 13 December 1962
and 2 January 1963
Model: Celia Hammond
Client: *Harper's Bazaar*

**69. Advertising shoot for
Woollands II, 1965**

Paris and London, July & 11 August
1965

Inscribed '1639/104' on reverse
Unique silver gelatin contact print
2½ x 2½ inches

70. Advertising shoot for Mary Quant Cosmetics, 1966

Inscribed '1739/3' on reverse
Unique silver gelatin contact print
2½ x 2¼ inches

London, 24 January & 17 February 1966
Agency: S & W
Client: Mary Quant Cosmetics

71. Grace Coddington, 1965
Fashion shoot for *London Life*

Inscribed '1676/1' on reverse
Unique silver gelatin contact print
2½ x 2½ inches

London, 6 October 1965
Model: Grace Coddington
Client: *London Life*

72. Joanna Lumley, 1966
Fashion shoot for Selfridges

Inscribed '1776/1' on reverse
Unique silver gelatin contact print
2½ x 2¼ inches

London, 25 April 1966
Model: Joanna Lumley
Client: Selfridges

Historic Prints

This intriguing selection of prints all
date from Terence Donovan's
lifetime, and were printed either by
him or under his supervision. Those
described as 'vintage' were printed
in the year following the date of the
shoot, while the others are later
prints probably made by Donovan
in the home darkroom he set up in
the late 1970s.

73. 'Thermodynamic', 1960
Fashion shoot for _Man About Town_

Photographer's copyright stamp on
reverse
Inscribed 'TD 519/9 Man About Town
October '60' on reverse
Silver gelatin print
12 x 12 inches
Illustrated: _Man About Town_, January
1961, 'Thermodynamic'
Literature: Martin Harrison,
_Appearances: Fashion Photography Since
1945_, London: Cape, 1991

Diana Donovan and David Hillman
(editors), _Terence Donovan: The
Photographs_, London: Little Brown &
Co, 2000 (unpaginated)

Grove Road Power Station, London,
31 October 1960
Models: Tim Davies
Client: _Man About Town_

74. 'The Secrets of an Agent' I, 1961
Men's Fashion for *Man About Town*

Photographer's copyright stamp on
reverse
Inscribed 'TD 639/3 Man About Town
March '61' on reverse
Silver gelatin print
12 x 12 inches
Illustrated: *Man About Town*, May 1961,
'The Secrets of an Agent'

London, 6 March 1961
Client: *Man About Town*
Model: Peter Begarty

75. 'The Secrets of an Agent' II, 1961
Men's Fashion for *Man About Town*

Photographer's copyright stamp on reverse
Inscribed 'TD 639/11 Man About Town
March '61' on reverse
Silver gelatin print
12 x 12 inches
Illustrated: *Man About Town*, May 1961,
'The Secrets of an Agent'
Literature: Martin Harrison, *Appearances:
Fashion Photography Since 1945*, London:
Cape, 1991

Another print of this image was
exhibited at *The Eye That Never
Sleeps – Terence Donovan – London
Photographs*, Museum of London,
17 March – 1 August 1999

London, 6 March 1961
Client: *Man About Town*
Model: Peter Begarty

76. 'The Secrets of an Agent' III, 1961
Men's Fashion for *Man About Town*

Photographer's copyright stamp on reverse
Inscribed 'TD 639/9 Man About Town
March '61' on reverse
Silver gelatin print
12 x 12 inches
Illustrated: *Man About Town*, May 1961,
'The Secrets of an Agent'
Another print of this image was exhibited
at *The Eye That Never Sleeps – Terence
Donovan – London Photographs*, Museum of

London, 17 March – 1 August 1999

Steps of the V & A, London,
6 March 1961
Client: *Man About Town*
Model: Peter Begarty

77. Advertising shoot for Acrilan, 1960

Photographer's estate stamp on reverse
Inscribed '305' on reverse
Silver gelatin print
16½ x 12¼ inches
Literature: Diana Donovan and David
Hillman (editors), *Terence Donovan: The*

Photographs, London: Little
Brown & Co, 2000 (unpaginated)

London, 25 February 1960
Model: Jan Williams
Agency: FCB
Client: Acrilan

**78. Advertising shoot for Signal
Toothpaste, 1960**

Inscribed 'Kodak, Exp. for Signal
Toothpaste (Foot Cone & Belding),
TD '90' on reverse of original mount
Photographer's stamp on reverse of
original mount

Vintage silver gelatin print
11 x 14 inches

London, 1960
Agency: FCB
Client: Signal Toothpaste

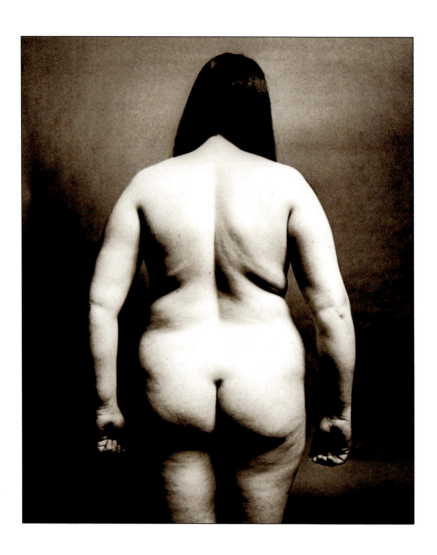

79. Beauty feature for *Nova*, 1969

Photographer's stamp on reverse of
original mount
Silver gelatin toned print
6¾ x 5¾ inches
Illustrated: *Nova*, June 1969

Literature: Diana Donovan and David
Hillman (editors), *Terence Donovan: The
Photographs*, London: Little Brown &
Co, 2000 (unpaginated)

London, 24 March 1969
Client: *Nova*

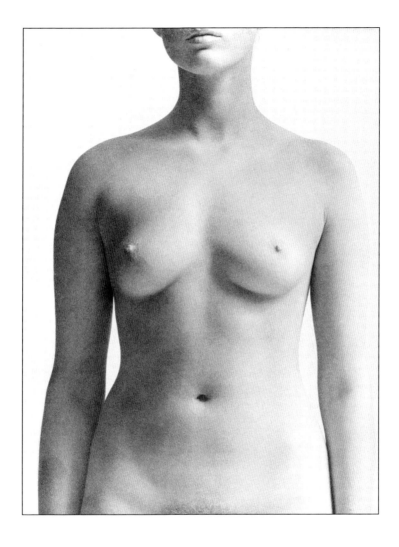

80. Nude study for *The Sunday Times Magazine* cover, 1967

Inscribed 'The Sunday Times cover 1967 12,000 printed then scrapped by photographer' on original mount
Photographer's stamp on reverse

of original mount
Silver gelatin toned print
14½ x 11 inches

London, 29 August 1967
Model: Marcia White
Client: *The Sunday Times Magazine*

81. Nude study for *Glances*, 1983

Photographer's estate stamp on reverse
Vintage silver gelatin print
9½ x 12 inches
Illustrated: Terence Donovan, *Glances*, London:
Michael Joseph, 1983, Plate 15

82. Nude, 1990

Photographer's estate stamp on reverse
Vintage silver gelatin print
9½ x 13¾ inches
Literature: Diana Donovan and David Hillman
(editors), *Terence Donovan: The Photographs*,
London: Little Brown & Co, 2000 (unpaginated)

83. Vanessa Angel, contact print, early 1980s

Photographer's estate stamp on reverse
Silver gelatin contact print
12½ x 11½ inches

84. Vanessa Angel, early 1980s

Photographer's estate stamp on reverse
Vintage silver gelatin print
12¼ x 16½ inches

85. Cindy Crawford for *Vogue*, 1988

Photographer's estate stamp on reverse
Vintage silver gelatin print
14¼ x 11¾ inches
Illustrated: *Vogue*, August 1988, 'Cut To
The Night'
Literature: Diana Donovan and David
Hillman (editors), *Terence Donovan:
The Photographs*, London: Little Brown
& Co, 2000 (unpaginated)

Bourdon Street, London, 26 April 1988
Camera: Pentax 6 x 7
Lights: 2 x Soft Boxes
APT: F8.75
Model: Cindy Crawford
Hair: Nicky Clarke
Make up: Mary Greenwell
Client: British *Vogue*

86. Room 251, Park Lane Hotel, London, 1988

Photographer's copyright stamp on reverse
Inscribed '3731 55' on reverse
Vintage silver gelatin print
16 x 11¾ inches
Literature: Diana Donovan and David Hillman (Editors), *Terence Donovan: The Photographs*, London: Little Brown & Co, 2000 (unpaginated)

Room 251, Park Lane Hotel
London, 6 June 1988
Camera: Fujica 6 x 8
Film: PX 120
Aperture: F 5.6
Speed: 1/4 second
Model: Michelle Geddes
Make Up: Martin Pretorious
Client: Italian *Harper's Bazaar*

87. Sir Ralph Richardson, Lord Olivier & Alec Guinness, 1980

Photographer's estate stamp on reverse
Inscribed 'TD 639/9 Man About Town
March '61' on reverse
Vintage silver gelatin print
19 x 15½ inches
Literature: Diana Donovan and David Hillman (editors), *Terence Donovan: The Photographs*, London: Little Brown & Co, 2000 (unpaginated).
Another print of this image was exhibited at *The Eye That Never Sleeps – Terence Donovan – London Photographs*, Museum of London, 17 March – 1 August 1999

Client: British *Vogue* (unpublished)

88. 'Pure Glamour', 1995
Fashion shoot for *Brides*

Photographer's estate stamp on
reverse
Inscribed '4152 AC3' on reverse
Vintage silver gelatin print
14 x 9½ inches
Illustrated: *Brides*, February 1996,
'Pure Glamour'

Park Lane Hotel, London,
31 August 1995
Camera: Fujica 6/8
Film: PX 120
Light: 2 x Bowens Spots
Model: Heidi
Hair: Kevin Graham
Client: *Brides* Magazine